Pathfinder 17

A CILT series for language teachers

Grammar matters

by Susan Halliwell

Cartoons by Caroline Mortlock

CILT

Other titles in the PATHFINDER series:

Reading for pleasure in a foreign language (Ann Swarbrick)
Yes - but will they behave? Managing the interactive classroom
     (Susan Halliwell)
On target - teaching in the target language (Susan Halliwell and Barry Jones)
Communication re-activated: teaching pupils with learning difficulties
     (Bernardette Holmes)
Bridging the gap: GCSE to 'A' level (John Thorogood and Lid King)
Making the case for languages (Alan Moys and Richard Townsend)
Languages home and away (Alison Taylor)
Being creative (Barry Jones)
Departmental planning and schemes of work (Clive Hurren)
Progressing through the Attainment Targets (Ian Lane)
Continuous assessment and recording (John Thorogood)
Fair enough? Equal opportunities and modern languages (Vee Harris)
Improve your image - the effective use of the OHP
     (Daniel Tierney and Fay Humphreys
Not bothered? Motivating reluctant learners in Key Stage 4 (Jenifer Alison)

Acknowledgements

I am grateful to Chris Abel, Keith Doman and Nicky Nesbitt for the examples from their teaching, and to Caroline Mortlock for her cartoons.

I would also like to thank the language learners who have talked to me about grammar and in particular Ruth Laxton who has allowed me to use examples from personal letters written to me in the early stages of her language learning.

First published 1993
Copyright © 1993 Centre for Information on Language Teaching and Research
ISBN 1 874016 12 7

Cover by Logos Design and Advertising
Printed in Great Britain by Oakdale Printing Co. Ltd.

Published by Centre for Information on Language Teaching and Research, 20 Bedfordbury, Covent Garden, London WC2N 4LB.

Contents

TEACHERS:

Tense is what you feel when you have to teach it.

I can't cope with functions, they are too amorphous.

There are no rules about word order in English.

You can say *der die das* quicker than you can say article.

Memo

There is a poster in room 10 advertising, in French, the delights of our city. It contains spelling mistakes and errors of grammar. Could you please have it removed since, despite the view of some of our colleagues that the presence of such work, however badly executed, encourages others, it seems to me to do precisely the opposite and is not presumably a fitting example of what you wish to see taught within the department. Could you make sure that similar inaccurate and ungrammatical work does not go on display.

The way I start the passive is with passive smoking.

I never really learnt grammar until I had to teach it.

I had one kid who thought things became feminine in the plural.

They have to believe they're getting somewhere. Even if it doesn't improve their German staggeringly, at least they feel they are doing something.

LEARNERS:

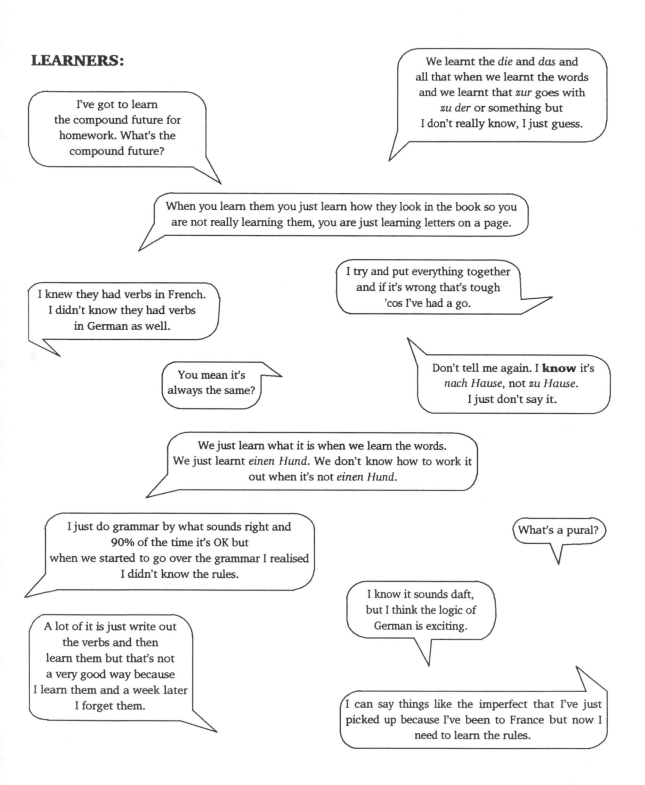

Introduction

Recent developments in language teaching have left many of us unsure what to do about grammar. Old approaches have been questioned, some would say discredited, and yet so far nothing clear has emerged to replace them. New approaches are being tried out but some people feel they are not working. Yet without any sense of pattern a foreign language is just a terrifying jumble. For the learner it is just an unpredictable collection of single items all of which have to be remembered in isolation.

How can grammar best be handled? Should we approach it directly or indirectly? Do we work with or without formal terminology? What can we base our decisions on? Is there any basis at all for choice other than fashion, instinct and personal preference? This Pathfinder sets out and explores some of the issues through practical examples. It is intended as a starting point for discussion.

Meanwhile, a new generation of language learners with more enthusiasm for other languages as part of their normal lives than we have ever seen before is moving through our schools. We owe it to them to sort out these questions. Grammar undoubtedly matters.

1. Grammar: What?

Different people use the word 'grammar' in different ways. Among other things, the word is used to refer to:

★ a description of a language and its constituent elements;
★ the terminology in which that description is formulated;
★ the rules to which the language operates;
★ the patterns created by those rules.

Grammar as description

Communicative approaches have brought about a marked shift in the way in which languages are described and categorised. We have seen a move from the focus on **form** to concern with **function**. A focus on form gives us lists and tables of such things as cases, tenses, noun declensions and verb conjugations and grammar guidance set out like this ...

2. PAST TENSE I

In Russian the past tense is not conjugated. It changes its ending according to the gender and number of the subject.

л is the sign of the past tense.

For the great majority of verbs the infinitive ending **-ть** is removed and **-л** is added to form the past tense masculine, **-ла** the past tense feminine and **-ло** the past tense neuter.

Infinitive		Past tense masc.	fem.	neut.
дýма – ть	to think	дýма – л	дýма – ла	дýма – ло
мы – ть	to wash	мы – л	мы́ – ла	мы́ – ло
éха – ть	to travel	éха – л	éха – ла	éха – ло
стоя́ – ть	to stand	стоя́ – л	стоя́ – ла	стоя́ – ло
бра – ть	to take	бра – л	бра – лá	брá – ло

We shall deal with the plural ending later. It is important to remember that there is only one past tense in Russian.

3. EXERCISE WITH THE PAST TENSE

а Я стоя́л, я брал мы́ло и мыл рýки и дýмал.

Да, ты стоя́л, ты брал мы́ло и мыл рýки и дýмал.

Starting Russian, BBC, 1962

... and produces work in exercise books which looks like this:

Le dix-huit octobre   Devoir

Page 37 Ex E

1 Il l'a volé. ✓

2 Il lui a parlé. ✓

3 Elles l'ont fait. ✓

4 Aurez-vous les regarder? ✓

5 Jamine ne l'adore-t-elle pas?

6 Il va le lui donner. ✓

7 Elle les leur offre. ✓

8 Ne l'as-tu pas invité? ✓

9 Lui avez-vous parlé ce matin? ✓

10 Elle les lui donne ✓

A $\frac{1}{3}$ ★

On the other hand, a focus on function means that a language is categorised according to the meaning it is used to convey. This also produces lists but they now look like this:

II General notions

1 Existential

1.1 existence, non-existence: there is ... (P); there's no ... (P); is there ...? (P); exist (P); make (P) *We ~ bicycles here.*

1.2 presence, absence: here (P); not here (P); away (P).

1.3 availability, non-availability: have/have got (P), used in affirmative and in negative contexts; there is ... (P); there's no ... (P); is there ...? (P).

1.4 possibility, impossibility (objective): possible, impossible, can, cannot (P) (see I.2.12).

1.5 occurrence, non-occurrence: happen (P).

1.6 demonstration: show (P) *Please, ~ me another one.*

2 Spatial

2.1 location: here (P); there (P); somewhere (P); (not ...) anywhere (P); nowhere (P); where? (P); everywhere (P); inside (P) *Put the car ~*; outside (P) *The children are playing ~*; the north (P); in ~ (P) *He lives ~*; the south (P); in ~ (P) *Bournemouth is ~*; the east (P); in ~ (P) *Norfolk is ~*; the west (P); in ~ (P) *There are beautiful beaches ~*; demonstrative adjectives and pronouns: this, that, these, those (P).

2.2 relative position: against + NP (P) *He stood ~ the wall*; at + NP (P) *We'll wait ~ the station/I bought this book ~ Colchester*; behind + NP (P) *There's a tree ~ the house*; between + NP (P) *He walked ~ two policemen*; in + NP (P) *I live ~ London/The letter was ~ the envel-ope*; in front of + NP (P) *There's a tree ~ the house*; next to + NP (P) *Please, sit ~ me at dinner*; on + NP (P) *The meat was ~ the table*; opposite + NP (P); outside + NP (P) *He spends most of his time ~ the house*; over + NP (P) *We flew ~ the city*; round + NP (P) *There's a wall ~ our garden*; under + NP (P) *The dog slept ~ the table*; with + NP (P) *I shall be ~ you in five minutes*; above + NP (R) *We were flying ~ the clouds*; among + NP (R) *We found a ring ~ the flowers*; before + NP (R) *There was a tree ~ the house*; below + NP (R) *We were flying ~ the clouds*; beside + NP (R) *Come and sit ~ me*; in + NP (R) *He's ~ the room above*; inside + NP (R) *I have never been ~ this museum*; at the end (P); ~ of + NP (P) *Turn left ~ the street*; at the side (P); ~ of + NP (P) *Put your car ~ the road*; in the centre (P) *I'd like to sit somewhere ~*; in the centre of (P) *The best shops are ~ the town*; where + sub-clause (R).

2.3 distance: distance (P) *The ~ from A to B is 5 miles*; near (P) *The village is quite ~*; near + NP (P) *We live ~ the cathedral*; far (away) (P) *The museum is not ~*; far (away) from + NP (P) *We live ~ the town*; in the neighbourhood (of + NP) (R).

2.4 motion: to move (P) *The car did not ~*; stand still (R); stop (P) *The car ~ped suddenly*; go (P) *The car would not ~/Why did you ~?*; get up (P) *I got up at six*; lie down (P) *I would like to ~ for an hour*; sit

I   Language functions

1 Imparting and seeking factual information

1.1 identifying: demonstrative pronouns: this, that, these, those + BE + NP(P); demonstrative adjectives: this, that, these, those + N + BE + NP (P); personal pronouns (subject form) + BE + NP(P); declarative sentences (P); short answers: *Yes, he is,* etc. (P).

1.2 reporting (including describing and narrating): declarative sentences (P); head-clause containing verb of saying (to say), thinking, etc. + complement clause (indirect speech) (P).

1.3 correcting: same exponents as above; in addition: no (adverb) (P); negative sentences with not (P); sentences containing the negation-words never, no (adjective), nobody, nothing (P).

1.4 asking: interrogative sentences (yes/no questions) (P); declarative sentences + question intonation (R); question-word sentences with: when, where, why, what (pronoun), which (pronoun), who, what (adjective), which (adjective), how far/much/long/etc. (P); whose (pronoun and adjective) (R); question-tags, type: *You aren't afraid, are you?* (R); tell me + sub-clause (P); about + NP (P).

2 Expressing and finding out intellectual attitudes

2.1 expressing agreement and disagreement

agreement: I agree (P); that's right (P); all right (P); of course (not) (P); yes (P); (yes +) affirmative short answers: it is, I am, I can, he may, etc. (P); certainly (R).

disagreement: I don't agree (P); I don't think so (P); no (P); (no +) negative short answers (P); that's incorrect (R).

2.2 inquiring about agreement or disagreement: do(n't) you agree? (P); do you think so, too? (P); don't you think so? (P); short questions (P).

2.3 denying something: no (adverb) (P); negative sentences with not (P); sentences containing the negation-words never, no (adjective), nobody, nothing (P); (no +) negative short answers (P).

2.4 accepting an offer or invitation: thank you (P); yes, please (P); I shall be very glad + V_{to} ... (P); that will be very nice (P); all right (P); with pleasure! (R).

2.5 declining an offer or invitation: no, thank you (P); I'm afraid I cannot ... (P); unfortunately I cannot ... (R).

2.6 inquiring whether offer or invitation is accepted or declined: will you + VP (*do it, come,* etc.) (P).

2.7 offering to do something: can I + VP (P); shall I + VP (P).

2.8 stating whether one knows or does not know something or someone: I (don't) know (P); $\sim$ + noun (-group) or pronoun (P).

2.9 inquiring whether someone knows or does not know something or someone: do(n't) you know? (P); $\sim$ + noun(-group) or pronoun (P).

**2.10 stating whether one remembers or has forgotten something or some-

5

The Threshold document from which the above extracts come was originally produced for the Council of Europe[1]. It is a version for schools of the earlier attempt by linguists to identify what meanings young mobile Europeans would need to be able to convey and understand in order to travel and work freely within the community as a whole and therefore across language boundaries. As we can see from the English examples above, this codification according to meaning/function instead of according to structure/form produces quite different groupings of language items from those familiar in traditional latinate grammars. For example, we can see clearly how one function or one notion can be conveyed in a variety of different forms, e.g. the notion of futurity can indeed be expressed by:

★ the future tense itself, i.e. *je demanderai*

but it is also familiar to us as:

★ simple present+adverb, i.e. *je demande demain*
★ *aller*+infinitive, i.e. *je vais demander*

Or, the function of refusing can be expressed in several forms ranging from a structurally simple and rather terse *Nein* to complicated and socially more subtle structures as *Es wäre mir lieber wenn ... nicht*.

Similarly, one structure like *ne ... pas* can appear as a key part of an enormous range of functions, e.g.:

★ refusing   *je ne veux pas*
★ disagreeing   *ce n'est pas vrai*
★ describing   *il n'a pas de ...*
★ instructing   *ne quittez pas*
★ expressing likes and dislikes   *je n'aime pas ...*

This way of looking at language in terms of the way we use it to communicate rather than in terms of its constituent parts has had a profound effect on our syllabuses and textbooks. Our National Curriculum documents mirror these changes, for example through their references to tense in terms of *'past, present and future actions'* (AT2;6)) or *'time references'* (AT2.8) and to such things as:

★ *'expressing feelings, likes and dislikes'* (AT2.3)
★ *'offering simple explanations'* (AT2.4)
★ *'giving simple descriptions of people, places, objects (e.g. colour, size)'* (AT2.2)
★ *'seeking and giving information, views and opinions'* (AT2.5)

1. Van Ek J, *The threshold level for modern language learning in schools*, Council of Europe, Longman, 1977.

In fact, in many respects the National Curriculum is only reflecting changes that were already under way in our coursebooks. Textbooks reveal the change from form to function by such headings as:

6.

Kein Problem

- problems of communication
- apologising
- ...and transport problems; asking for help

Wieviel Uhr ist es? Wie spät ist es?

What's the time?

This unit is about arranging to meet people; this section teaches you how to tell the time in German, ...hat you can agree on when to meet someone.

Parlez-moi encore un peu de votre famille

Objectifs

How to say what the members of my famil... are called

How to say how old the member... family are

How to understand extr... about the family

TES OBJECTIFS

In this unit, you will learn how to ...

... invite someone to go somewhere
Ça te dirait d'aller à la piscine?
On pourrait aller au musée?

... react to something good or bad and say how you feel about it
Génial!/C'est super!/Zut alors!/Ce n'est pas juste.

... react to someone else's feelings
Tu as raison/Ne t'en fais pas.

HOW TO
ask and talk about preferences
...and how to find a friend

In this unit you will find out how to do these things in French:

ask someone what they are looking for
tell them where it is
tell someone what you are looking for
ask someone where something is
tell the time (as long as the clock has stopped at twelve!)

Indeed one textbook refers specifically to the threshold level:

Vous y êtes?

Experts in the Council of Europe have spent many years working out what you need to learn in a foreign language to enable you to move freely from one country to another. For many languages, including French, they have worked out what you need to be able to do in the language to be able to go to that country to live and to work. They have called this the 'Threshold Level' because, once you have reached it, you are ready to step into the foreign country and its way of life. Are you on the threshold for French? Find out by filling in this questionnaire: it has been produced for the Council of Europe by one of its experts as a way of letting people find out if they have reached the Threshold Level.

Instruction: Imagine that you meet a French-speaking person from another country. He does not know anything about you or your country. Indicate your estimated command of the language by putting a cross in the appropriate box (*Yes* or *No*) for each statement.

		Yes	No
1	I can tell him when and where I was born.	☐ Yes	☐ No
2	I can spell my name in French.	☐ Yes	☐ No
3	I can describe my home to him.	☐ Yes	☐ No
4	I can tell him what kinds of food and drink I like and don't like.	☐ Yes	☐ No
5	I can tell him about my interests (hobbies, interests in general. etc).	☐ Yes	☐ No
6	I can tell him what I usually read (kinds of books, newspapers, magazines, textbooks, etc).	☐ Yes	☐ No
7	I can ask him what newspapers there are in his own country.	☐ Yes	☐ No
8	I can tell him what I do in my free time.	☐ Yes	☐ No
9	I can ask him how to get to a certain place by public transport.	☐ Yes	☐ No
10	I can tell him what I think of art galleries.	☐ Yes	☐ No
11	I can ask him about the price of a ticket for a certain football match.	☐ Yes	☐ No
12	I can tell him about things that might interest a tourist in my home region.	☐ Yes	☐ No
13	I can ask him questions about traffic-rules in his own country.	☐ Yes	☐ No
14	I can say something about social security in my country (old-age pensions, medical care, etc).	☐ Yes	☐ No
15	I can tell him what sort of government we have in my country.	☐ Yes	☐ No
16	I can say something about my political views and tell him whether I support a political party.	☐ Yes	☐ No
17	I can tell him how I feel at the moment (if I am hungry, tired, ill, etc).	☐ Yes	☐ No
18	I can ask him to help me arrange an appointment with a doctor.	☐ Yes	☐ No
19	I can tell him that I take medicine regularly.	☐ Yes	☐ No
20	I can tell him that I am tired and need some rest.	☐ Yes	☐ No
21	I can ask him to repeat slowly what he just said.	☐ Yes	☐ No
22	I can ask him about the pronunciation of a certain word.	☐ Yes	☐ No
23	I can ask him to characterize the climate in his country.	☐ Yes	☐ No
24	I can ask him if he knows the approximate price of a certain piece of clothing in his own country.	☐ Yes	☐ No
25	I can inform him about where he can have his car serviced.	☐ Yes	☐ No
26	I can ask him to ring me up some time.	☐ Yes	☐ No
27	I can ask for his telephone number and give my own number.	☐ Yes	☐ No
28	I can tell him where he can change foreign money.	☐ Yes	☐ No
29	I can describe weather-conditions in the four seasons in my own country.	☐ Yes	☐ No
30	I can tell him where he can eat and drink.	☐ Yes	☐ No
	Total number of crosses:	— Yes	— No

Evaluation: If your total number of Yes crosses is (25) or above, and if your judgement of your own language ability is fairly accurate, you are likely to have reached Threshold Level in French.

Action, Book 4 (Thomas Nelson)

Examination syllabuses also reflect the change. Sometimes the result is cumbersome and produces rather strained headings such as *'stating whether something is considered a logical conclusion'*. It is interesting that the same syllabus from which this phrase comes also has a section called *'Structures and grammar'*. This reflects a potential problem with the functional/notional approach. The problem, particularly for those of us brought up on a traditional latinate grammar, is that this functional/notional approach may be a very interesting way to explore language, but as a basis for teaching it can often seem far too diffuse. For example, different parts of a verb may appear in different units, or adjective endings may crop up without being 'dealt with'. Textbook writers try to get round this with varying success by little minisummaries of structural grammar points.

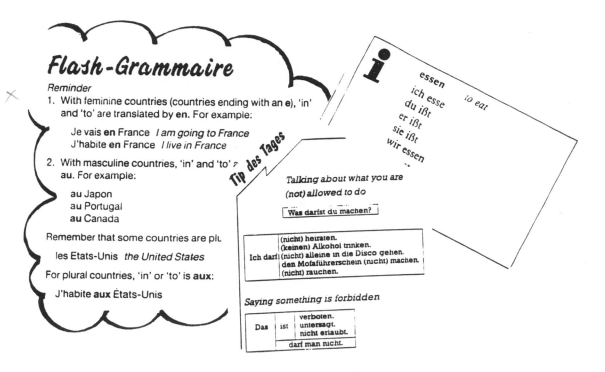

Flash-Grammaire

Reminder
1. With feminine countries (countries ending with an e), 'in' and 'to' are translated by **en**. For example:

   Je vais **en** France *I am going to France*
   J'habite **en** France *I live in France*

2. With masculine countries, 'in' and 'to' a ... **au**. For example:

   au Japon
   au Portugal
   au Canada

Remember that some countries are plu ...

   les Etats-Unis *the United States*

For plural countries, 'in' or 'to' is **aux**:

   J'habite **aux** États-Unis

Tip des Tages

Talking about what you are (not) allowed to do

| Was darfst du machen? |

| Ich darf | (nicht) heiraten. (keinen) Alkohol trinken. (nicht) alleine in die Disco gehen. den Mofaführerschein (nicht) machen. (nicht) rauchen. |

Saying something is forbidden

| Das | ist | verboten. untersagt. nicht erlaubt. |
| | darf man nicht. | |

essen
ich esse
du ißt
er ißt
sie ißt
wir essen

to eat

The danger here is that, in trying to compensate for the diffusion, teachers can find themselves trying to introduce items in bulk which are not backed up by the text. This is a situation which is usually very trying for teachers and pupils alike. There is also a temptation to resort to formal terminology in a halfhearted or haphazard way which can create more problems than it solves.

Grammar as terminology

> *They wouldn't know a verb if it hit them on the head.*

To which some people would reply: yes, they would. In their mother tongue they do not muddle verbs up with anything else. Indeed, they create new ones which follow all the 'rules'. So the problem is not the verbs or any other language elements themselves, but the way we use the labels for them.

Terminology or no terminology? The main advantage is that it provides a very convenient shorthand for referring to grammatical elements. Many of us have struggled with clumsy phrases like 'doing word' or even more cumbersome 'the word which stands in for the word you have just referred to ...'! On the other hand, it is surely no help for learners to be introduced to such homegrown terminology as 'definite and indefinite gender' (sic!). Nor for textbooks to use the terms inaccurately. One popular textbook states misleadingly that *'the word tense is used to mean the time when an activity takes place'*. It then goes on inaccurately to give as an example:

● We use verbs in the **future tense** to say what we're going to do:
   Example:
   I'm going to watch (the news).
   Je vais regarder (les informations).

Another textbook uses the terms possessive pronouns and possessive adjectives interchangeably. In some people's eyes this is acceptable but it will do little to help the learners understand the different nature of pronouns and adjectives. If we are going to use formal terminology then we ought to have a clear idea of what we are doing.

It is also worth reminding ourselves that there is nothing inherently wrong with technical terms. One five-year-old, after listening patiently while an adult explained laboriously how *'we cut one shape in cardboard so we can keep drawing round it and make sure we get exactly the same shape each time'* announced: *'You mean we need a template'*! The word 'verb' like the word 'template' is in itself not a difficult word to cope with if it is used as a label for something already experienced or known.

The problem for us here then is not so much the terminology itself as the level of abstraction it usually creates. In addition, there is the danger that because the terminology allows learners to talk about the language, that is what they learn to do. As previous generations discovered to their cost, we may find that pupils use the labels to discuss the language but cannot produce spontaneously the language those labels refer to.

Grammar as rules

Grammar rules are simply a descriptive codification of the inner workings of a language. They are rules in the sense of observed patterns, like the 'laws' of science. In this respect, as guidelines for action and prediction, grammar rules are immensely helpful. But there is one main problem of getting at language and communication from the rules. It can be very complex to work out even a very simple message from the rules.

HOW THE LANGUAGE WORKS

VERB STEMS

The *Keywords* section of this unit lists the new verbs you have learnt – words for 'go', 'do' etc. They are listed in two ways – as *stem* forms like **jaa** and **kar**, and also with endings like **jaataa, jaatii** or **karte**. The stem form is the most basic form of any verb to which endings like **-taa**, and others you will learn in later units, are added. Normally any new verbs will be listed in *Keywords* in their stem form.

AN 'ONGOING SITUATION' – THE HINDI AND URDU -taa FORM

The Hindi and Urdu **-taa** form, a bit like the English '-ing' form, is added to a verb stem to refer to an *ongoing* and *uncompleted* activity or happening. So, if you ask someone **aap kahãã kaam kar*te* hãĩ?**, or **aap kahãã rah*tii* hãĩ?** you're assuming that they're still work*ing* or liv*ing* somewhere. The **-taa** form is not always best translated as *-ing* however. Because it can also refer to a *habitual* activity or a *mental state of affairs* (unlike English '-ing') it is often better translated into English 'simple present' tense:

mãĩ Tren mẽ jaatii hũũ	I go by train.
I train -in going am	

mãĩ Muhammad Ali **ko jaantaa hũũ**	
I Muhammad Ali -to knowing am	
	I know Muhammad Ali.

The **-taa** form changes to agree in *number* and *gender* with the person you are talking about – the *subject* of the sentence. (Remember from Unit 1 that **aap** is plural in order to be polite even if you are talking to one person):

Resham:	**mãĩ kaar mẽ aataa hũũ.**	(Masculine Singular)
Rena:	**mãĩ** Bordesley Green **mẽ rah*tii* hũũ.**	(Feminine Singular)
Anita:	(to Dr Shah) **aap kyaa kaam kar*te* hãĩ?**	(Masculine Plural)
Javad:	(to Vijay) **aap vahãã kaise jaa*tii* hãĩ?**	(Feminine Plural)

These are the shapes the **-taa** form takes:

	Masculine	Feminine
Singular (e.g. **mãĩ**, 'I')	**-taa**	**-tii**
Plural (e.g. **aap**, 'you')	**-te**	**-tĩĩ***

* **-tĩĩ** becomes **-tii** when it is followed by **hãĩ**, as in all the examples we have seen so far.

Hindi Urdu bol chaal, BBC, 1989

12

To take another, much simpler example, this time from French: *je voudrais*, which is so quickly learnt as a whole phrase, is formed by taking the future stem of the verb (which in this case, just to confuse matters, is irregular) and adding the imperfect endings! Or, to take an example from German: the simple message that my little brother is in the kitchen at the moment doing the washing up '*Im Moment spült mein kleiner Bruder in der Küche ab*' contains decisions on:

★ the cases of three nouns;
★ case endings for three genders;
★ a 'strong' adjective ending after the possessive adjective;
★ word order after a non-subject beginning to the sentence;
★ tense;
★ form of the third person singular of the verb;
★ word order with a separable verb ...

So, a simple message tackled like this is a complex exercise. That is why some teachers prefer to focus on pattern rather than terminology.

Grammar as pattern

You mean it's always the same?

It is the 'grammar as pattern' approach which produces this kind of chart in textbooks ...

Haben Sie	**einen** Stadtplan?
Möchten Sie	**einen** Prospekt?
	eine Broschüre?
Was gibt es hier zu sehen, bitte?	
Es gibt Sie haben	**den** St. Johanner Markt. **die** Ludwigskirche. **das** Museum.

Meine Lieblingsfilme sind Ich sehe am liebsten	Krimis. Komödien.
Western Lustige Filme	kann ich nicht leiden. hasse ich.

... and which led a PGCE student to devise the following prompt for generating sentences which practise word order:

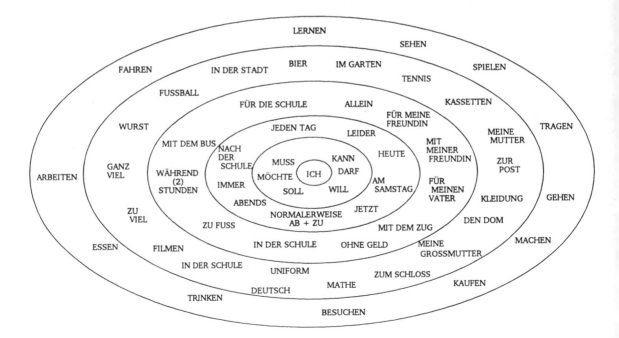

14

This is probably the most common way of thinking about grammar at the moment, but it has certain implications. If the emphasis is on pattern, then that pattern has to be obvious whether attention is drawn to it or not. The problem with the examples above is that you probably cannot see the pattern unless you already know it. The presented pattern allows you to generate accurate language, but it does not teach you the pattern itself for future reference. This battleships grid for practising time/manner/place/word order in German is designed to overcome that by providing repetitive use.

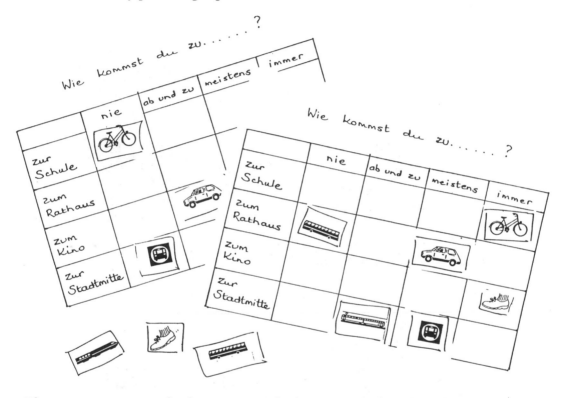

The more we expect the learners to take in pattern indirectly, the greater is the need for exposure to that pattern in use. There is a very interesting and frustrating paradox here which is not always acknowledged. We have two elements within the communicative approach which tend to pull in two different directions. We have a focus on how the language is actually used for communication, i.e. a functional/notional grammar, and at the same time a belief in acquisition of language by subconscious assimilation of structural pattern. The problem is that a functional/notional approach tends **not** to produce sufficient repetitive structural pattern, at least not within the limits of two hours or so exposure a week. This is at the root of some of the present confusion and it forces us to look at the role of acquisition and learning and how each contributes to a grasp of grammar.

15

2. Grammar: How?

Grammar direct or indirect?

We do not set out to learn our mother tongue. We pick it up as we go along, through exposure to it and through the need to use it. We do not lose this instinct and ability to 'acquire' a language, as we discover if as adults we are immersed in another language community. Stephen Krashen[2] and others contrast this automatic and subconscious process with conscious 'learning' of a kind most familiar from traditional language learning in school. At the risk of over-

---

2. Krashen S D *Second language acquisition and second language learning*, Pergamon, 1981.

simplification, the essential differences between the two processes can be summarised as follows:

Learning	Acquisition
★ conscious	★ subconscious
★ applies rules	★ senses rules
★ seems quick	★ seems slow
★ concerned with form	★ concerned with function
★ focus on the language itself	★ focus on the message
★ rewards carefulness	★ rewards risk
★ correction crucial	★ correction potentially inhibiting
★ communication only as goal	★ communication also as process

Both the direct process of learning and the indirect process of acquisition are acknowledged in the National Curriculum. The Non-Statutory Guidance refers to the way in which *exposure to the target language ... supports pupils' language acquisition without overt teaching* (C1.6). At the same time, in the programmes of study under the heading *Developing language learning skills and awareness of language*, we find the statement that pupils should have regular opportunities to *use knowledge about language (linguistic patterns, structures, grammatical features and relationships ...) to ... develop their own use of language*.

The interesting question for most teachers is how the two strands, the two processes of learning and acquisition, relate to each other.

The most controversial area of Krashen's work has been the model he developed as his 'monitor theory' to describe this relationship (1981). He suggested that what we have consciously learnt provides a controlling monitor for what we have subconsciously acquired. As he pointed out, there are those who overuse the monitor and tend to get stuck in working out the rules at the cost of uninhibited communication. In contrast, there are others who, as it were, underuse the monitor and communicate happily without bothering about accuracy. The optimum users in his terms are those who can use the rules in situations where accuracy is appropriate, but who can also switch off the monitor in the interests of fluency. This monitor model has not met with general acceptance[3] as a 'fact' but it has great appeal for classroom teachers for several reasons. Not only does it tie in with the experience most of us have both as teachers and as learners ourselves, but it gives a necessary and complementary role to **both** acquisition and learning in the process of getting a grasp of a language. As the introduction to the National Curriculum programmes of study says, pupils should take part in activities which *help them to acquire, learn and use the target language* (page 21)

---

3. McLaughlin B 'The monitor model: some methodological considerations', *Language learning* vol 28, part 2, pp 309-331.

(though in passing it is worth pointing out that to phrase the idea like this is misleading since it separates 'use' from 'acquisition'. In fact, we acquire through use).

In terms of our classrooms, this duality of learning and acquisition:

★ allows for different temperamental approaches to language learning;
★ allows for differences of ability relating to age and intellectual stage.

Above all,

★ it gives us good reasons for being flexible in our approaches and provides principles on which to base our choices.

This potential for informed flexibility is reflected in the three practical examples below.

Different approaches in practice

There seem to be three main approaches to grammar teaching in circulation. Each has its advantages and disadvantages, its gains and losses. Which approach each teacher chooses will have more to do with those gains and losses and the consequent appropriateness to the particular situation than with any fashionable 'correctness'.

The lessons below come from the regular repertoires of three teachers and, with minor adjustments, are as the teachers wrote them. The lessons have been chosen not because they are the only possibilities open to us, nor because they represent right and wrong, but because they illustrate clearly three very different styles in practice. The comments in italics are those of the teachers themselves.

Approach 1: grammar presented and practised implicitly

Teaching point: *devoir* + infinitive

'This activity is for Year 9 pupils. They use Tricolore 3 *as a basic course book; but this is one of my own supplementary lessons. This "lesson" actually takes between one and two hours depending on the ability of the group. It covers four activities using the skills of listening, reading and guided writing. It builds on pupils'*

imagination and creativity. It is designed to establish the pattern of devoir+*infinitive. It is also intended to provide some fun. The pupils will previously have learnt sequence words such as:* d'abord, puis, après, après ça, ensuite *and* finalement'.

Part 1		- listening to instructions whilst watching demonstration - reconstructing events from written instructions

Vous devez
=
you must

i.	Introduction	'Vouz devez écouter et vous devez regardez. Dans mon sac j'ai ... un concombre, ... une carotte, des ... pique-saucisses et des ... raisins de Corinthe'.

On OHP

ii.	Demonstration	Make crocodile as if doing TV cookery demonstration, making sure instructions are delivered slowly and are repeated. The instructions to be given in the same order as the worksheet. Keep it simple. Pupils watch and listen.

Pour faire un concombre crocodile

Vous devez prendre: ★ un concombre   ★ des pique-saucisses
                     ★ une carotte   ★ des raisins de Corinthe

Méthode

D'abord vous devez couper le haut du concombre en biais pour faire la tête.

Puis vous devez couper le concombre en fines tranches pour faire le corps.

Après vous devez découper une fente dans le concombre pour faire la bouche.

Après ça vous devez découper une langue dans la carotte.

Puis vous devez mettre la langue dans la bouche.

Ensuite vous devez fixer les yeux avec des pique-saucisses.

Après vous devez découper quatre pattes dans la carotte.

Finalement vous devez attacher les pattes au corps.

Et voilà - un concombre crocodile!

---

iii.	Sorting the instructions	*'Maintenant vous devez arranger les phrases'.* One worksheet (precut into strips and in an envelope) is given to each pair of pupils. Use OHP to demonstrate how the pupils rearrange the strips to reconstruct the order of events.

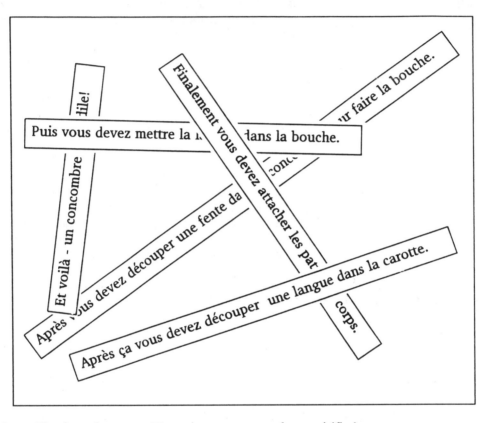

iv.	Check and copy	*'Et maintenant vous devez vérifier'* Check with OHP and then pupils copy instructions from their worksheet into their books.

Part 2		- making an animal - writing their own instructions

i.	Pupils design own animal	*'Aujourd'hui vous devez faire un animal'.* Distribute to each pupil one potato, one carrot, some cocktail sticks and plenty of currants (some will be eaten!). Each pupil designs an animal of their own choice.

ii.	Write instructions	Pupils write their own instructions using the previously copied version of the crocodile instructions as model.
iii.	Photos	Photos are taken of the resulting animals, written work is checked, and copied out neatly (see p22). Photos and instructions are then mounted for display.

Comment

'One great advantage of the approach is that it appeals to all ability levels. They all receive the same input through the demonstration, and the visual element supplies what they do not know linguistically. The commentary and the peripheral instructions reinforce the pattern naturally. The jumbled written instructions, once they have been sorted, provide the model from which to work when they write their own. The important point is that every child irrespective of ability can produce some instructions for themselves. These will range from the simple to the more ambitious.

It is important when doing the demonstration to keep the language very simple and to highlight at every possible moment the pattern of vous devez+infinitive. The peripheral instructions such as vous devez regarder ... vous devez écouter... etc help to reinforce this too. One disadvantage of this activity is that only the vous form is learnt, but this can be overcome by doing other activities (such as battleships) at a later stage when the variation of the verb forms can be highlighted. At this stage the intention is to establish the basic pattern, and in this respect the approach is very effective.

Another disadvantage might seem to be that at the demonstration stage the pupils have nothing to do but watch and listen. In fact, this has never been a problem. Indeed, they usually sit in amused silence whilst the demonstration is taking place. They do not know what the outcome is going to be until the final ... et voilà ... un crocodile! The remaining activities involve them actively.

All in all the activities provide plenty of practice to establish the pattern, some of the final products are delightful ... and we all have fun doing it.'

une chouette

1 pomme de terre.
1 carotte
raisins de corinthe
pique - saucisses.

1 D'abord vous devez c
pomme de terre.

2 puis vous devez cou
tranche de carotte
pour les ailes

3 Après ça vous de
une fente dans l
faire le bec

4 Après vous deve
raisins de cori
pique-saucisses
yeux
et voilà

Pour faire un Éléphant.

Ingrédients.
1 pomme de terre
1 carotte
raisins de Corinthe
Pique-saucisses.

Méthode.
1.   D'abord vous devez couper quatre morceaux de carotte pour les jambes et les mettre dans la pomme de terre avec des pique-saucisses.
2. Puis vous devez couper un morceau de carotte pour la tête ensuite vous devez la mettre dans la pomme de terre avec des pique-saucisses.
3. Ensuite vous devez couper des tranches de la carotte pour les oreilles et la trompe et les mettre dans la tête avec des pique-saucisses.
4. Ensuite vous devez mettre les yeux avec des raisins de Corinthe et des pique-saucisses.
5. Finalement vous devez fixer un morceau de carotte pour la queue.

Et voilà un Éléphant !

Approach 2: explicit grammar practised as pattern

Teaching point: the perfect tense with *avoir*+ER verbs

'I do this with Year 8 mixed ability. Prior to this lesson I would have revised **avoir** *in the present tense so that pupils are familiar with its sound and pattern. The class knows* avoir *as a pattern so I use a verb "spider" to drill the parts.*

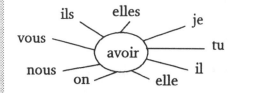

The advantage of practising a verb like this is that you can "dot" about very quickly without having to resort to English or terminology. Pupils can also use these to "test" each other.'

Part 1

i.   Demonstrate   *hier* and *aujourd'hui* using days and dates.

Hier (le 2 juin)	Aujourd'hui (le 3 juin)
un sandwich au fromage	Je mange un sandwich au jambon
Eastenders	Je regarde Neighbours
au tennis	Je joue au football
mes cassettes	J'écoute la radio

ii.   Present pattern   *Aujourd'hui je mange un sandwich au jambon.*
                           Hier j'ai mangé un sandwich au fromage, etc.

iii.   Build up drill   Pupils listen first time.
                           Pupils repeat (whole class).
                           Do as drill in 'open pairs' (i.e. pairs across the class not with their immediate neighbour):
                           Pupil A: *Aujourd'hui ...*
                           Pupil B: *Hier ...*
                           Swap roles.

iv.   Strengthen   by adding word cards to board: *j'ai mangé, j'ai*
       visual pattern   *regardé, j'ai joué, j'ai écouté.*

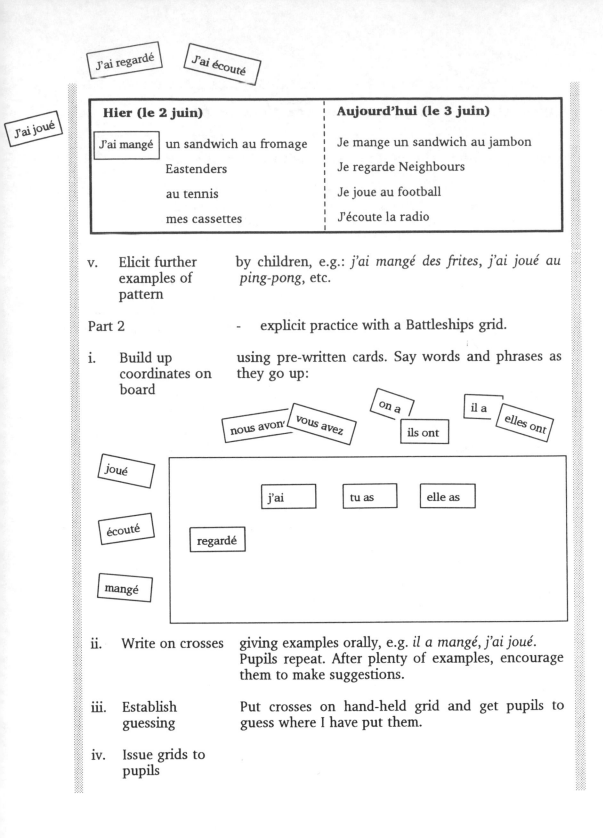

J'ai regardé

J'ai écouté

J'ai joué

Hier (le 2 juin)		Aujourd'hui (le 3 juin)
J'ai mangé	un sandwich au fromage	Je mange un sandwich au jambon
	Eastenders	Je regarde Neighbours
	au tennis	Je joue au football
	mes cassettes	J'écoute la radio

v.   Elicit further examples of pattern

by children, e.g.: *j'ai mangé des frites, j'ai joué au ping-pong*, etc.

Part 2   -   explicit practice with a Battleships grid.

i.   Build up coordinates on board

using pre-written cards. Say words and phrases as they go up:

nous avons   vous avez   on a   ils ont   il a   elles ont

joué

écouté

mangé

regardé   j'ai   tu as   elle as

ii.   Write on crosses

giving examples orally, e.g. *il a mangé, j'ai joué*. Pupils repeat. After plenty of examples, encourage them to make suggestions.

iii.   Establish guessing

Put crosses on hand-held grid and get pupils to guess where I have put them.

iv.   Issue grids to pupils

le passé composé	j'ai	tu as	il a	elle a	on a	nous avons	vous avez	ils ont	elles ont
regardé									
mangé									
écouté									
joué									

v.   Demonstrate   using one pair of more able pupils.
      Battleships game

Each pupil puts a specific number of crosses on his/her grid, e.g. one on each line. Pupils take turns to find their partner's chosen squares by saying a phrase which gives the coordinates. If they guess the position of one of their partner's crosses correctly they have another turn.

Comments

'I recently found this method particularly effective when teaching a mixed ability class which included five low ability pupils, as it involves intensive structural repetition within an active and communicative activity. It's also great fun! I was able to listen in on every game while every pupil had the opportunity to practise the structure. Informal discussion and presentation of the pattern avoided the use of formal terminology which would have been incomprehensible and inaccessible to most pupils. It is also possible to conduct this discussion in French, i.e.: regarder ... notez la différence ... présent ... passé ... je mange ... j'ai mangé ... écoutez la différence encore une fois ... présent ... je mange ... passé ... j'ai mangé.'

The danger of this approach as a whole lies in practising the pattern in isolation and out of context. However, in a later lesson the same grid could be used for written practice, with the class actually writing the phrases in the squares. Pupils could then refer to the grid when completing a cloze exercise requiring the use of those verbs.

In my experience the advantages outweigh the disadvantages as the pattern is used repeatedly by even the least able pupils and forms a sound basis for future exploration of this tense.

Approach 3: explicit grammar formally discussed

Teaching point: imperfect/simple past in German

'I would expect to use the following with the top 25% of the ability range - those expected to achieve A-C GCSE - at the beginning of the fourth year when they would already have come across the perfect. I use Deutsche Heute.

I see the advantages of the approach in its rapidity and completeness: at least in theory pupils should be able on the basis of this to form the simple past tense of any verb in the language. It is a good area of grammar to demonstrate the productiveness of pattern recognition and rule application. It is intellectually challenging even for brighter pupils but with careful thought they can produce answers which are 100% correct and can have a sense of achievement.'

Part 1

i.	Name and function	**Explain** why the name 'imperfect' is a poor (and for pupils taking French, confusing) name since while it is an entirely appropriate and useful name for its function in French, 'simple past' is a better description in German. Explain when used.
ii.	Strong/weak	**Explain** that the most important distinction in the simple past is between strong and weak verbs. **Give definition** of strong verb. **Explain** that given the connection between English and German the weak/strong definition exists in English too: walk/walked, sing/sang (or perhaps a digression into American English preserving now obsolete strong forms dive/dove, sneak/snuck).
iii.	Pattern/form	**Set out pattern** for weak verb on board using different coloured chalk for endings, reminding class of the watch/watched parallel. Quick **oral practice** with easy weak verbs to encourage confidence.
		Write strong verb alongside the weak with vowel change also in a different colour:

kaufen: to buy	**singen**: to sing
ich kauf-t-e	ich sang
du kauf-t-est (notice similarity)	du sangst
er kauf-t-e	er sang
wir kauf-t-en	wir sangen
Ihr kauf-t-et	Ihr sang-t
Sie kauf-t-en	Sie sang-en
sie kauf-t-en	sie sang-en

iv. Separable/   **Revise** the separable prefixes - write list on board.
     inseparable   **Give examples** of sep./insep weak verbs, e.g.: *einkaufen/verkaufen*; sep./insep. strong verbs, e.g.: *aufstehen/verstehen*.

v.   Word order   **Give examples** of sentences to show that word order is the same as for the present.

kaufen: to buy

ich kauf-t-e
du kauf-t-est   (notice similarity)
er kauf-t-e
wir kauf-t-en
Ihr kauf-t-et
Sie kauf-t-en
sie kauf-t-en

singen: to sing

ich sang
du sangst
er sang
wir sangen
Ihr sang-t
Sie sang-en
sie sang-en

Ich	*kaufe* → *kaufte*	in der Stadt ein
Er	*verkauft* → *verkaufte*	sein Haus
Wir	*stehen* → *standen*	um 8 Uhr auf
Sie	*verstehen* → *verstanden*	meine Frage nicht

vi. Reference   **Explain** how they can find out whether a verb is
     grammar   strong or weak, how the textbook shows this and where to find information, i.e. in vocabulary sections verbs are given in the form *stellen* (weak) or *schwimmen* (i,a,o)+refer them to the verb tables.

Explain why all compounds of a verb cannot be given. **Emphasise** that there are a few verbs which are so irregular that they have to be learnt by heart, e.g. *bringen/brachte* (perhaps the occasion to bemoan the fact that natural languages rarely exhibit perfect patterns).

vii. Quick exercise

There must be practice within the lesson **manipulating** the above information. Using the information in their textbooks, they should practise forming simple pasts from infinitives:

1. *machen (er) > er machte*
2. *finden (wir) > wir fanden*, etc

viii. Homework

To learn the patterns and re-read notes.

Part 2
- Follow up

This rather abstract treatment obviously needs to be backed up with more extensive contextually based practice, e.g. gapped exercises or guided construction of a narrative passage with simple past question forms as stimuli.

Comments

'There is an obvious danger in this approach that pupils will not be able to use spontaneously what they have learnt: that it risks becoming an unreal exercise (like solving simultaneous equations, say) which has little to do with real communication. To overcome this, it is essential that there is plenty of follow up work in which pupils **use** the tense.

Set against these disadvantages are the advantages mentioned above, of rapidity and completeness. In addition, there is the fact that this approach allows the learners to be self reliant and gives them independent access to formal grammar reference material whether in the textbook or in the dictionary.'

These three approaches are so very different from each other that it needs to be stressed that none of these teachers uses exclusively the approach offered here. In fact, each of them could probably have supplied one or both of the other versions. But what is clear from conversation with all three of them is that they make informed choices about which approach is appropriate when, and having made those choices have identified clearly what features they need to incorporate in the teaching. It is particularly significant that all three approaches have certain aspects in common. In different ways:

★ they all break the work into manageable stages;
★ they all provide very considerable repetition of the pattern;
★ they all support sound with vision, or vision with sound, and the board or the OHP have a key role to play in this;
★ they all provide ample opportunity either in speech or in writing for the learners to handle for themselves what they are learning.

3.   Grammar: Which approach and for whom?

As we saw in the examples above, each of the three teachers has made a personal choice based on professional insight about when one approach is more appropriate than another. Those choices will rest primarily on:

★ the language elements concerned;
★ the learners themselves

Choice according to the language elements concerned

Different elements of a language lend themselves to different treatment. The way relative clauses operate in German is an example of a pattern that is difficult to talk about succinctly, but like the earlier word order grid in German for time/manner/place (on page 14) it is a pattern that can easily be 'felt' through repetitive pattern practice in use. Here is an example of a partially completed listening grid which is then used for paired conversation and finally as the basis for constructing sentences. So far the teacher has said:

Der Stuhl, der im Wohnzimmer ist, ist neu.
Die Lampe, die im Keller ist, ist kaputt. etc.

Once completed, the grid is used for paired conversation, e.g. partner A turns the grid over, partner B uses the grid to test A's memory:

Der Stuhl, der im Wohnzimmer ist, ist neu, nicht wahr?

It is significant that it is a grid again, and provides a useful reminder of the value of schematic prompts to strengthen pattern.

	der Stuhl	die Lampe	das Bild	die Gardinen
im Wohnzimmer	neu			
im Schlafzimmer		neu	schön	
im Keller		kaputt		
in der Küche				alt

On the other hand, there are some aspects of grammatical manipulation for which most learners find it enormously helpful to have a straightforward checklist or mnemonic. For example 'Drapers van MMT' is fairly common as a reminder of the first letters of the French verbs which take *être* in the perfect.

So, different elements of structural grammar will lead us to choose different approaches on different occasions. As the teacher who provided the potato monster lesson for practising *devoir*+infinitive said:

> *'For example, indirect speech in German is extremely complicated. It is usually done very quickly and with an entirely explicit grammatical explanation. If I have bright pupils who are considering doing 'A' level I aim to teach them this complicated structure directly.'*

So, obviously, the ability and temperament of the learners will also affect our choice of approach.

Choice according to the learners concerned

It is obvious that we should build on the instincts, skills and preferences that learners bring to the classroom. However, we also need to remember that we have a responsibility to extend and add to those skills and instincts. So, taking the learner into account also means helping them to develop new and different skills. Thus the 'blurters' need help working on conscious accuracy and the cautious 'workers-out' need encouragement to go for fluency.

There are of course some choices which are clear. The twelve-year-old who worked hard to produce this in his mother tongue:

I get to school my fens are they bell go's the and
every body go's in to they fom room to be recaeid.
ble go into the room for the fost lesen have
a his go's the bell go's. hofe howe and the full
kind bell go's it is dreck the dreat lasts have
the bell go and it we go of the next lesen

was not going to benefit from an approach to grammar which relied both on the
capacity to handle abstract rules and on the skills of reading and writing. But
other choices are not so easy. The ability to handle overt grammar is not a fixed
state nor is it just the product of ability to attend to detail. As the following
extracts show, individual learners will shift from easy accuracy and conscious
attention to detail to a mixture of inadequacy and apparent carelessness. These
were real family letters, not school exercises, but they reveal clearly how
competence fluctuates ...

★ ... between stages ...

Féiier le 23

Chère Susan,
        Merci de la lettre. J'adore le grand
cochon Je suis dans la salle a manger.
Je travaille ò la table. A New Brighton il fait
froid et il pleut. Quel temps fait il a Norwich?
    Aujourd hui je porte: une jupe noir, un tricot
noir, une cravate noire et blanche, des chassures
noires et des chassettes noires. C'est tout noir!!!

?? ?? blanche!
une cravate
un tricot

une jupe

des chassettes
des chassures

Maman joue le violin.
    A bientôt

Ruth xx

le trente et un décembre

Chère Susan,

Merci beaucoup de ton cadeux. C'est dans ma chambre mais il n'ai pas une fleur maintenant! Maintenant je suis dans le salon avec grand-père. J'ai mal à la main parce-que cet après-midi j'écris six lettres. Ils disent 'merci beaucoup pour...' et ils sont très, très longues. Nous avons eu un très bon Noël dans New Brighton. Qu'est-ce que tu fais dans Botswana pour Noël? C'est chaud? J'ai beaucoup de bonnes cadeux. Maman et Papa donne moi le papier pour le dessin (très grand), quatre ✎ pour le dessin (Qu'est que c'est en France), et £30!! Ça fait pour ma ordinateur (C'est un très petit ordinateur n'est pas) J'ai mettre de côté et dans 1990 je vais de l'argent de côté mai l'argent de poche. C'est un très bonne idea n'est pas.

Hier nous (Sarah, Maman, Grand-père et moi) sont allons à Lurddas pour visité mes autres grand parents. Le dernier jeudi nous avons visité Ray, Brigdet, Emma et Alastair.

Le prochain jeudi nous allons aller à l'école. C'est terrible! Ce mois nous allons choisi les G.C.S.E.. C'est très difficiles parce que j'aime beaucoup soixante matières. Je peux fais huit et l'etudes général, au neuf. Qu'est-ce que tu fais pour 'O levels'? Maintenant je vais jouer de piano et mange le dîner.

A bientôt,

et Bonne Année, 1990,

et Grosses bises

Ruth

33

★ ... between languages ...

DANKE. SCHON. MERCI BEAUCOUP

Chère Susan,

Merci beaucoup pour nos vacances fantastique. Tu est très, très gentille. Nous avons eu les meilleurs vacances à "half-term" de nos vie. Le voyage a était très de fond mais nous avons joué le "Master Mind" et nous avons écrit un lettre de dix pages à une amie qui s'appelle Denise.

Es ist Sonntag heute darum habe ich nichts zu viele zu schreiben. Mutti, Vatti und Sarah haben ihren Gedanke gern.

Heute habe ich an meine Deutsche Freundin und meine belgisch Freundin geschrieben. Donnerstag, ich muß eine musik Untersuchung haben (Theory Grade) Ich weiße die Antworten nichts!

Ich habe das Papair in "Elm Hill Craft Shop" gekaufen.

Kate sagt viele, viele danke auch.

Schrieb schon

Devi Ruth

★   ... and depending on the extent to which the writer is trying to communicate or just concocting a letter out of phrases she knows ...

22/8/90.

Liebe Susan,

Wie ghts'? Mir gehts' gut. Letze Woche ich bin noch Taunton gefahren. Ich bin mit der Zug gefahren. Ich habe ein gut Ferien gehabt.

Letze Samtag ich bine an der Alter Towers mit meine freundin gefahren. Es was heiß. Wir sind mit eine siebenundzwanzig Bus gefahren! Sie heißt Bertha. Wir haben an der Black Hole und der Corkscrew ge ∿∿∿ !!

Morgen Mutti und ich gehe noch Chester. Ich will eine ⌂ gekaufen.

Das ist meine fünfte Brief ich habe geschrieb hier. Ich habe zwei Brief auf Frankreich, und zwei auf der U.K geschrieb.

In zwei Woche der Schule beginnt!

Ich hoffe

Schreib!
Lebe!

Schreib mir noch mal bitte,

Ruth

Der 'Black Hole'
in der Schwarze

35

... and finally there are the differences in competence between spoken and written accuracy which produce such oddities as *'le sol est brie'*, or will lead a learner to write *je mange* for what he or she says perfectly accurately as *j'ai mangé*.

Luckily there are some fixed points in these shifting sands. For example, personal experience suggests that:

- all learners benefit from grammar through acquisition;
- younger learners acquire more readily than they learn;
- all learners need to learn how to learn consciously;
- slower learners can appreciate the routines of simple grammar;
- the transition from learnt rules to spontaneous speech is beyond many learners;
- we cannot take the transition from accurate speech to accurate writing for granted.

If you consider the above statements and the earlier ideas and examples, both in the light of your own experience and in discussion with other teachers, two aspects of this issue will emerge very clearly.

1. There is no single approach which has all the answers.

2. It does not help to mix the approaches in the same activity. They undermine each other.

Our choices must be deliberate, informed and flexible if we are to get it right.

4.   Getting it 'right':
points for reflection, discussion and action

So what, in these circumstances, is right? In teaching as in politics it is possible to become trapped into perceiving one set of choices and values as 'correct' as in the sense of publicly acceptable. This has been happening very noticeably over the issue of grammar teaching. In mother tongue English teaching there is currently tremendous pressure, though mainly from outside the profession, to return to conscious formal grammar training. In foreign language teaching, interestingly enough, the trend is going the other way and we have the spectacle of teachers feeling guilty about 'old fashioned' explicit grammar methods. It did not come as any surprise that the teacher who supplied the examples on pages 26-28 at first refused, saying it would *just be held up to ridicule*. 'Pedagogic correctness' of this kind does not help anyone, neither learners nor teachers. Good grammar teaching is not a question of professional rights and wrongs. It is a balancing of effects, needs and the kind of informed flexibility which comes from constant analysis, experiment and discussion. Seen from this angle the differences in process and product between more overt and more covert grammar teaching are not problematic, but enriching. They enable each of us to assess and respond more effectively to the wide range of temperament and competence which we encounter in our classrooms.

So, finally, some starting points:

As a department we can ...

- establish the range of approaches, and the principles behind them, which exist within the department. What picture/experience of grammar are the learners getting? (The three examples in this book could provide a starting point for discussion.)

- compare and agree on which, if any, formal terminology or informal substitutions for terminology is used to describe patterns.

- discuss how to introduce formal terminology, if at all:
  - which ability level?
  - which age level?

- find out what the learners have to say about grammar. How does what we think we are doing match up with what they think is happening? Their remarks can be very revealing (see speech bubbles at the front of the book).

- consciously monitor the effect of different approaches. If two members of the department teach parallel classes, experiment with different approaches for a particular unit:
  - explicit/implicit;
  - mainly through speech and listening/ mainly through reading and writing;
  - with/without terminology.

- brainstorm on ideas for teaching specific structures, e.g. *celui-ci* etc.

- share ideas for use of OHP or other visuals to demonstrate pattern.

- build up a collection of support materials:
  - grammar games;
  - worksheets;
  - wall posters;
  - materials for independent learning, revision and reference.

- ask learners to help us devise grammar games (board games and card games make a good starting point) and wall posters.

- make some mini grammar-explanation videos if there is a video camera in the school. These can either be used for self reference by learners or could be used in class across the department.

- consult with the English department over:
  - terminology;
  - similarities and differences;
  - timing;
  - using examples from each other's subjects;
  - a joint or coordinated grammar awareness course possibly as part of a wider language awareness programme.

- design your own departmental grammar awareness lessons or part lessons.

As individuals we can ...

- ask ourselves as we plan and teach 'How can I, for this group and this language element, best maximise pattern?'. The following checklist may help:

    pattern signalled: e.g.   'heading' on board ... *'today's lesson is about ...',*
    'heute machen wir ...', 'Bon, à la page 45 ...
    regardez le petit diagramme ... c'est ça qu'on va

faire aujourd'hui ... maintenant fermez les livres et écoutez ...'

pattern seen:	e.g.	on the board/OHP/wall chart/in their exercise books/emphasised by gesture,

- words and phrases grouped;
- highlighted through colour, size, movable cards.

pattern heard:	e.g.	emphasis/volume/significant pauses ... used as part of the general instruction of lesson '*... on va écrire et puis on va ... tu vas? ... je vais*'.

pattern felt:	e.g.	tapped out rhythms, chanting, actions. Drills have a role here too.

pattern explained/ discovered:	both backed by as many of the above as possible.

and above all,

PATTERN USED IN REAL COMMUNICATION.

5. Further reading

From English as a foreign language

Harmer J, *Teaching and learning grammar*, Longman, 1987.

Ur P, *Grammar practice activities: a practical guide for teachers*, CUP, 1988

The examples in both these are naturally both based on English grammar but the ideas are usefully transferable.

From mother tongue English

Carter R (ed), *Knowledge about language and the Curriculum* (the LINC reader), Hodder and Stoughton, 1991.

From the modern foreign language world

Johnstone R, *Communicative interaction: a guide for language teachers*, CILT, 1989.

Chapter six is particularly helpful on this topic.

From the field of language awareness

Hawkins E, 'How language works', chapter 6 in *Awareness of language*, CUP, 1984.

Jones B, *How language works*, CUP, 1984.

This book by Barry Jones is a topic book for pupils. It is one in the 'Language awareness' series of which Eric Hawkins was series editor.